The
Cineaste

The
Cineaste

A. Van Jordan

W. W. Norton & Company | New York · London

For information about permission to reproduce selections from this book,
write to Permissions, W. W. Norton & Company, Inc.,
500 Fifth Avenue, New York, NY 10110

For information about special discounts for bulk purchases, please contact
W. W. Norton Special Sales at specialsales@wwnorton.com or 800-233-4830

Manufacturing by Courier Westford
Production manager: Anna Oler

Library of Congress Cataloging-in-Publication Data

Jordan, A. Van.
[Poems. Selections]
The cineaste / A. Van Jordan. — First edition.
     pages cm
Includes bibliographical references.
ISBN 978-0-393-23915-7 (hardcover)
1. Motion pictures—Poetry. I. Title.
PS3610.O654C56 2013
811'.6—dc23

                              2012050216

W. W. Norton & Company, Inc.
500 Fifth Avenue, New York, N.Y. 10110
www.wwnorton.com

W. W. Norton & Company Ltd.
Castle House, 75/76 Wells Street, London W1T 3QT

1 2 3 4 5 6 7 8 9 0

for my family
in our love for film

CONTENTS

Metropolis, restored edition   15

I

Stranger Than Paradise   19

Last Year at Marienbad   21

The Red Shoes   23

Nosferatu   25

Un Chien Andalou   27

Killer of Sheep   29

The Mack   30

Pather Panchali   34

M   35

Rififi   37

The Great Train Robbery   38

The Brother from Another Planet   40

II

The Homesteader   47

Silent. I showed a patron to her seat   47

And I'm a Negro who can make it grow   48

My body's sky; they try to pick a star   49

Of the dangers I avoided of lust   50

First, I want the past to lie down and die   51

Real-life scenes strike fear, while past scenes just
   taunt   52

Birth of a Nation brings a love story   53

Just a hint of sweat, Agnes, on your breast   54

To survive this war with my girl's husband   55

Man, forget all the laws; we're in love and grown   56

Through the night, unrests breaks. How to
   survive?   57

Like hands folding into fists, the people   58

With shoes on feet and prayer on tongue, I drive   59

I proved man could choose art over the knife   59

Looking ahead pushes the past deeper   61

Others die complacent, eating crumbs from   61

All of the dead ascend to family   62

But what else should we try to fulfill? Work   63

I need the vibration of people in   63

As the story unfolds beneath my hands   64

But here I am, working, like it or not   65

I see you when I look outside, daily   66

Daily, I look outside and I see hell   67

Men and women have some stories to tell   68

Even at a movie, I keep my mind   69

Their shadows are cast from the light falling   70

Their bodies already lie at rest. What   71

Listen, after these new taxes are paid   72

I knowed hell and I had nothin' to lose   73

To slumber Wednesday night, at peace, dreaming   74

Bootblacks. Scared maids. Unknown hands on
    Sunday   75

Starting now, focused, I see through a lens   76

Sharpen the focus in your lens, and you   77

As the light bounces back and as the shot   77

In just one shot, I could offer a kiss   78

Pull in. Time for the close-up: the money   79

I need money to get started. Novels   79

I'll cast characters from *The Homesteader*   80

Starting now, the film we've all been waiting   81

Used to a life without hugs, not even   82

Mama says you have to fall on hard times   83

Even in death—Hollywood's star-lined streets   84

Night: In a city under the North Star   85

By train the bent-back sharecroppers come, too   86

III

Do the Right Thing   89

Run Lola Run   91

I've Heard the Mermaids Singing   94

Black Girl   96

American Gigolo   98

Blazing Saddles   101

Westworld   105

The Cabinet of Dr. Caligari   109

Ikiru   111

The Red Balloon   113

One Week   116

Oldboy   118

Acknowledgments   121

Notes   123

Nothing is lost, nothing wholly passes away, for in some way or another everything is perpetuated; and everything, after passing through time, returns to eternity.

—Miguel de Unamuno, *Tragic Sense of Life*

The
Cineaste

Metropolis, restored edition

(Michigan Theater, Ann Arbor, September 14, 2010)

Listening to the organist play feels like eavesdropping
inside the mind of a giant, a bipolar giant
whose emotions are so fragile I want to climb
up her arm to lay my hand on her shoulder.
The screen has yet to capture the first gray glimpse of skyline.
Music envelops the theater, enclosing the city
in a throat filled with indifference,
a city under a chiaroscuro of sunlight and shadow imagined
by those working in the depths of the metropolis—
a sort of giant, too, with some real issues to work out.
I remember watching, as a child in downtown Akron,
Wild Oscar play the organ, ascending from beneath the stage
at the Loew's Theater, long before it was renamed
the Civic Theatre, and even longer before it needed restoring
to save its life. Wild Oscar would play before the feature
or during the silent Krazy Kat shorts preceding
the main event. Going to the movies
seemed monumental: live music, opening acts, serpentine
lines around the block. When Oscar played,
I wonder, now, if he was happy or
was he beneath the stage the whole time
toiling like the workers in the film tonight,
preserving a magic moviegoers still believe in,
the way voters and lovers do not. Like many children,
I believed I would do something with my potential
once I simply grew up. Like many adults, I

stayed a child; potential hanging around like a shadow.
But every now and then, like tonight, I catch up
with my shadow self, and show up in a theater
to see a restored edition of an old film
about workers holed up in a factory for too many hours
and lovers separated, like most lovers, by their ideas.
One worker steps off line, reprieved by a brother worker,
and suddenly the sky appears, and the whole
rectilinear contraption—and I mean their lives, not just the plant—
comes tumbling down, an arcade of beliefs
in ruins. I wonder what it all means
to this audience, whose laughter rings a bit
condescending in the cued moments of melodrama.
It's so easy to laugh at the banana peels laid before the lives of others.
Sad to see the young act too old to feel naïve,
no suspension of disbelief. Not me.
Movies provide my last safe playground.
Tonight, for instance, when the organist descends to play,
and the lights expire, and the projection whirrs to action,
I'm as excited as a boy again. When the organ ascends,
what am I but as dazed as the workers climbing
from the depths of the metropolis—a little disappointed,
filled with questions, wondering how will I go on
with my day's work outside in all that natural light?

I

Stranger Than Paradise

(Jim Jarmusch, 1984)

Arriving in the New World, I discover
when you land someplace new,
everything feels the same. I've kept in touch
with my American family through letters
written in Hungarian. Meeting them,
speaking English, holds home at arm's length:
My cousin's one-room apartment shows me
all I need to know of Manhattan, so
I seek the shaded skyline of Cleveland
as a gift to myself. My cousin offers me a dress
as a token of acceptance, but it's ugly,
and I let him know I appreciate his ugly offering,
but, once out of sight, I pitch it in the trash
around the corner—my last act of love in the city.

Why do they call these meals TV dinners,
when we eat them at the kitchen table?
The road ahead will offer more questions
as answers. I welcome the Midwest smog
as clarity of where I am, for once. Snow
makes Lake Erie look like a painting.
What I mean to say is how it looks matters
less than how I feel standing before it.
My Aunt Lotte worries about my hanging
with bad boys, meaning her son and

his friend. Why not worry about them hanging
with me and my man, Screamin' Jay Hawkins,
who's a real bad dude, not to be messed with?
I can handle myself any place from Cleveland
to Cape Canaveral, from Budapest to the Lower

East Side, so back off and let me work
a spell on you. I've been headed toward
paradise my whole life. I've been on this journey
meeting strangers who mistake me for someone
they owe, and I accept their offerings
with wit and suspicion.
What else does a traveler need to survive?
Whatever comes my way, I share
with those around me, those people
calling themselves friends, cousins. I
see they need a guide on their journey,
someone to push them out of their homes
onto a plane, a beach, a road leading nowhere
holding promise—but promising, nonetheless—
a place they always said was nice, and promised me
I'd love, though they've never been there themselves.

Last Year at Marienbad

(Alan Resnais, 1961)

A place, though visible, is like a ghost
of memories. Even memories one forgets
linger in the space in which they occurred.

Here within the expanse of vaulted ceilings,
doorways leading to more doors, hallways
leading to more halls, the faintest recollections

absorb over time; no act will wholly evanesce.
Wander over the carpets and marble floors,
and the echoes of bygone eras endure,

wafting through corridors
like a perfume pulsing on a woman's neck.
What should one make of what happens

or doesn't through a night between lovers?
And if the space awakens in a man or a woman
some thing they would not find the inner charge

to commit in their own bedroom,
should they forget? Embrace this longing?
This couple, let's say, met last summer at a château

soirée, and they made love or they thought
about making love to each other. If they did make love,
well, they're adults, they'll turn to each other

in memory, forever waiting there for each other; they will
always have this place and time. If one evening
this couple, which is not really a couple,

lies together in one room while their lovers wait
upstairs or at home, if they both *thought* about making love
to each other, while glancing across a crowded room . . .

Well, why would anyone try to forget that?
Again and again, the moment is captured
in one's mind, but try to prove it happened,

and details retreat into darkness.
Again and again, *footsteps get absorbed by carpets,*
so thick, so heavy . . . Oh, how moments call, but better senses

abate any emerging pleasure. One may even convince
the body, against the will, that such moments were made
to linger, only awakened by the promise of possibility.

The Red Shoes

(Michael Powell, Emeric Pressburger, 1948)

Through the silence, the shoes are a night
without a body to share a bed with, while

a storm builds outside the bedroom window. Naked
is she without her red shoes; red

is the sky in the dream of the shoes at her feet.
A woman is a woman without red shoes

laced on her arched feet, but the shoes dance
whether she laces them up or not.

The woman who is not a dancer will dance
once she laces the shoes on her arched feet,

once her feet are arched in the shoes, red
will be the color of her toenails and the soles

of her feet. But what of her soul? That soul will be laced up,
too, and the dance will be a dance of a night in bed

with a lover through a storm. The need to dance
is the same as the need to live, without questions,

without knowing the next step. The need takes
the lead in the dance to the next stage, to the next lover

until the dance is all she knows, all she needs.
Yes, the shoes lead to a door inside her;

the door opens a room she didn't know existed.
Once inside, she dances the dance of no return,

a threat she refuses to heed, a space she must explore,
closing the door behind her, on the woman

she believed she was before the shoes kept beat to a tune
to which she hangs on for life, barely keeping up.

Nosferatu

(F. W. Murnau, 1922)

Evening on some lost corner of the Carpathians
renders shadows much in the way my hometown
of Akron did in my youth, when my taste

for the nocturnal planted desires
for what dark settings offered.
Those poor Carpathians never suspected

the Midwest as the source of their troubles.
As a child, I wanted to strike fear and find love,
once I grew up, but what boy doesn't?

Some acts don't play out well
during the day, when neighbors peer
through blinds, spying your approach.

Don't believe what you may have heard.
I did try to resist a décolletage in my day.
And at 745 years old, I can hardly blame

others for my mistakes. Some pieces
are not meant for the puzzle of my heart
to solve. Call me what you may—

Nosferatu, Dracule, A. Van—but
the other Van, the good Dr. Helsing,
pointed out in *The Book of Vampires*

what I couldn't comprehend: The cure
for my bite lies in the blood of "a woman,
pure of heart." I read the lines myself,

years before Helsing was even born, but here
I am, caught between a woman and a sunrise;
as I see the hint of light rising

over the mountains, I choose to stay.
Instead of striking fear through
another night, I roll over into her

embrace, leaving—for all she will remember—
the scent of smoke from one of her dreams.

Un Chien Andalou

(Luis Buñuel, Salvador Dalí, 1929)

Because a razor cuts across a frame of film,
I wince, squinting my eye,
and because my day needs assembly
to make sense of the scenes anyway,
making a story from some pieces of truth,
I go outside to gather those pieces.
Thousands of moments spooling out
frames of mistakes in my day.
As if anyone's to blame,
as if anyone could interpret the colliding
images, again and again, dragging
my imagination behind me,
I begin assembling.
I don't know anything, so I seek
directions, following the path
of ants from your palm, out
the apartment door to a beach.
Is this where I'm supposed to ask
if my hands on you bend
some light around shade? Maybe
I'm not ready for the answer. They say
art imitates what we can sculpt or write
or just see when we turn ourselves
inside out. I can't turn my eye away
from the sight of failure. The rain pelts rooftops.

I listen to the song, thinking
when the sun comes back,
beating down the door
in my head, I'll salvage whatever sits
still long enough for me to render,
before anyone knows what really happened.

Killer of Sheep

(Charles Burnett, 1981)

Men with the gentlest hands,
men with boys at home, with wives
to love, rise every day to work
in the slaughterhouse, draining
their own blood, daily, just to make an honest case
for their misery. It's beautiful to behold
endurance in the worker who knows love
motivates more than money. Sometimes the thought
of a woman's knee above a shaven calf, the thought
of his finger making circles on her knee,
while she sits next to him on a couch is enough . . .
Men learn as boys how a pile of rocks
can build a castle worth defending,
how when riding a bike, falling
can even be called play. By the time he's a man,
he knows what it takes to lift
a car engine up three flights of stairs:
it takes more than two hands, which just
seems part of pain's scheme. Even
a little boy, when it's all recalled later
as a man, wanted someone to scold him,
so a bloody job will one day satisfy
more than fast money, so
he knows to seek help to find a smile,
when all the day offers grimaces back.

The Mack

(Michael Campus, 1973)

Whether a little boy who grows
into a pimp, or a young girl who

becomes a ho, they both
hold in memory a mother

framed in a front door, calling, nightly,
for them to come into the house.

But The Game calls, too, and what man
or woman can resist an open hand extended

in the middle of a night? Cliché
comes to mind, maybe, when you think

of the pimp with a heart of stone,
but consider this an act to conceal

the weakness in his conscience,
which science has yet to study.

The young girl, now a woman, will
act, too, as a comfort to him or

she'll choose another. And when the other
man reminds him, *You know the game, nigga;*

Yo' bitch chose me, what more can he do
but offer a threat to conceal the boy

inside, who remembers he has a mother
calling him into the house? What can she do,

this young woman, but remember how pretty her
mother's face was, framed in the doorway?

Though she remembers the screen door
striking closed behind her mother's voice,

she stayed out. Why didn't they just head home
when the streetlights buzzed on? Too late

for questions now. By the time grown
folks are talking, all hope is lost.

These are niggas with money
problems; that is, their *pockets*

Look like they got the mumps. Some
brotha is talking unity in the black

community, calling the pimp
into the house, calling the ho

off the corner before those streetlights shine
down on her face. What does this brotha know

about life at the top? Blackness
now is just fodder for race theory later. But

today, *Goldie*, the pimp, hands out money
to kids who stay in school. He's the *Mack*

of the Year, but his ass is confused, too,
if he doesn't hear the mothers calling

for his head on a stick, which he'll
probably think is just a cool cane.

Poor, pastel-suit-wearin' muthafucka. Pimp,
you ain't no hero, so take off

your cape. Sista, listen, even a blue-collar
worker knows, at the end of the week,

you gotta pay *yourself*, first.
There may not be any food in the house

for the young girl, there may not be a TV
in the house for the little boy, but stop looking

at your poop-butt friends when I'm talking to you.
Stop asking questions when grown folks are talkin'.

You need to bring your young self home, even if you
think there's nothing there waiting on you. *Boy,*

git your ass in this house, and leave those girls alone!

Pather Panchali

(Satyajit Ray, 1955)

When a child dies before you do, remember:
Forget this pain. But keep her laugh, a totem to remember.

It's spring. The rain pelts the forest leaves like tears falling
down a mother's face; she tries not to remember.

In the *Jatra*, the brother protects his sister from the cold.
The actors onstage sing their story, so you'll remember.

Why steal a banana or jack fruit? Even the Devil's Apple couldn't
cure her fever. Fruit belongs to all, but too few remember.

In Kaash fields, we ran for the train, laughing, out of breath,
Kans grass whipping our ankles . . . Do you remember?

The path winds long, and the path to love often brings strain;
endurance calls for more than shoes for your journey, do remember.

Stay strong on the road, prepared for any storm ahead;
the path is a line in your palm, little *Apu*, remember.

M

(Fritz Lang, 1931)

Although it's quite dark now, the city
invites me to look for you. The people
disappear, for the most part, into homes

or taverns or into one another, into the night.
You know, white space proves most dangerous
at night. Bodies stand out like museum pieces

to ogle. I love museums, even during the day,
when women, filled to the brim with beauty,
walk through the galleries, staring

with such curious intent. I love staring, too,
at how the most public spaces turn
intimate after dark. Why do the trees look

so alert under moonlight? Almost as
if they witness my every move. I love
trees; they never give up, do they? People,

clouds, buildings—the trees don't care
about what anything else does, they simply do
what they came here to do. I've learned

so much from their example . . . And, yes,
I know you in the audience wonder when
I will say *"Wer weiß, wie es ist, ich zu sein?"*

in my broken German, but Peter Lorre
couldn't be here tonight, so I come,
proving a worthy understudy. Perhaps

you hoped to witness his penchant
for the young, like an accident you didn't
cause but of which you still feel a part,

a natural penchant to play voyeur. My tastes
differ, preferring to watch the mature at play,
learning from their adventures. But, please,

here I am, no translation necessary. Allow yourself
the freedom to imagine, to fantasize as you wish;
feel in me, day by day, each guilty,

God-discriminating touch come to a chord
struck beyond your body's will to seize
an opportunity only guilt kept you from taking.

Rififi

(Jules Dassin, 1955)

They take as men are wont to do—with zeal,
like men who want more from the world,
which sounds like a noble endeavor,
but when they plan, their plans involve
hurting others, if necessary, like men
will do when they desire. And every building,
every storefront window or locked door,
every vault with jewels or an open door,
or even a cop on a beat guarding a building,
forms a means to an end. The world fills with men
who want more, which sounds ignoble when plans involve
hurting others. When men with an endeavor—
men with patience, with skill—can hurt the world,
they do. They take, as men are wont to do, with zeal.

The Great Train Robbery

(Edwin S. Porter, 1903)

So much to take in then,
and so hard to imagine now.
The close-ups, the eyeliner,

spirit gum under mustaches,
all caught in the flash,
all revived in retinas. I look

and want to recall the first look
through the camera's focus,
sharpening against Edwin Porter's

eye socket, but the view offers
an innocence I cannot experience. I try
again wanting to recall the first glow

from the balcony, a year later,
sharpening against a Negro viewer's
skin, but the view offers

a danger I no longer can face.
The story unfolds from another story
as all stories do. I don't know

how the first light projected in the dark
struck a couple on their first date,
watching stories flash in their eyes,

images no one in attendance could say they saw
before, but I do know about trying
to duck before the bullet finds

its mission in this life, faster, closer
than seems possible until facing its dark eye.
And what about it? Don't laugh at the fear

of the man next to me, leaping from his seat,
but ask yourself, how long you could focus
your eye on your own approaching destruction?

The Brother from Another Planet

(John Sayles, 1987)

I see no sign of slavery in this city of Harlem;
no city on this planet could thrive tethered to pain
for long, not with its alleys and after-hour joints to scream in:
a quadrant whose design holds mysteries, shibboleths,
and idioms. In the streets, life-forms "walk" on leashes
cared for by those tugging the leashes,
scooping up excrement behind them. Their behavior
bends through my mind like voices breaching
a boarded-up window. I see no place
where the Men in Black could blend in with inhabitants;
though some inhabitants resemble them, and look
equally lost in the city; both stand out as lost men, trying
to find a way out. I plan to cast a shadow
alongside those who accept me; our shadows cast
the same darkness. Some are flung against walls,
some are thrown to the ground. All the same darkness.

Question: Do our shadows make us equals in light?

I'm an alien to those around me, though we
look alike . . . they search my face . . . they call me brother:
They say, *The brother has a way with machines, but he's short
on words.* They say, *The brother just wants to sit in peace, man.
Leave him alone.* But I want to stay among those who
call me *brother*, not left alone. I understand what they mean

when they talk, though I cannot speak their language;
I can only reply with deeds, which they seem to appreciate.

Question: Why do they even speak, when words fall short?

I've escaped, it seems, to a home in which I've never lived.
Though the possibility of this seems nil, or, at least,
illogical. I explore to see how close I can come
to a proof . . . I make friends . . . I make love . . .
I care for those I have never met . . . Time passes . . .
Soon, I notice my three-toed feet are not like theirs.
When I hear a woman singing, I fall in love.
I cut my onyx toenails to make her a necklace.
When I offer it to her, she accepts,
she smiles. Her palm fits inside mine
like a girl holding her father's hand. Finding a boy inside me,
I smile, too . . . Time passes . . . One day, down an alley,
I find a boy with a needle in his arm; his body still.
I pull the instrument from his vein,
insert it into mine. I see my shadow peel off the ground.
I feel my shadow walk away from me . . . Time passes . . . I awaken
to begin my mission: find The Source of this joy that also harms.
I observe, but I hear someone's mother say, *It's rude to stare*,
so I walk away, leaving my right eye in a potted plant . . .
Time passes . . . Night:

I come to retrieve data from my eye.
I set out to track The Source.

Question: What god makes a love one cannot put down,
          even as it destroys?

I recognize the potential for drudgery. Years ago, I escaped
slavery on my planet. The skills I used to escape,
I'll use now to stay free. These skills
adapt well to my new home, where brotherhood
is a language. Those who don't know its alphabet
soon feel the jarring of earth beneath them . . . I locate The Source . . .
The Source has not consumed the substance
he releases through the city. I smother him in its
acquired taste. The skills I used to escape, I use now
to help others stay free. But by *getting involved*,
which is how I heard a man in the Lenox Lounge describe it,
I expose myself. The Men in Black find me . . .
I run . . . I fight back . . . I keep running . . .
Local brothers try to help, but they are not equipped.
I run . . . I fight back . . . A quiet comes over the city.
Time passes . . . I keep running. I enter alleys,
after-hour joints, but, by getting involved,
I discover that the city does have brothers like me,
brothers who acquired skills while escaping

from other planets. Over the course of the night,
as I face the Men in Black, these brothers find me,
stand beside me, remembering how they came to this city,
how they came to stand in sunlight, came to discover snow.
The night is brilliant with brothers like stars
scattered over the city. How they light up the streets,
the alleyways! How they stand beside me to fight,
though muted, and though love fuels every one of them.

II

The Homesteader

(Oscar Micheaux, 1919)

FADE IN

INTERIOR TRAIN—1902

Pullman porter OSCAR MICHEAUX, while en route to Chicago
from Cleveland, overhears passengers talking about homesteading
land in South Dakota and Nebraska.

Silent. I showed a patron to her seat.
She traveled alone, walking behind me.
And though I heard her heels, I held my eyes.
She had nothing to say, just greeted me
With ticket shoved in my palm, intimate
It almost felt, but distant with silence.
Just as one train car leads to another,
So her walk through coach led her to talking
To others about a Rosebud homestead,
A new farming town of Gregory, new
To white men, at least; Lakotas tilled land
There years before. I read of land to claim,
Land to claim for any man man-enough
To make it grow, Negro or white alike.

. . .

And I'm a Negro who can make it grow.
Once I got word of what I needed, I
Turned my own train around. I had to know
The joy of owning my own land. My eye
Trained on the future, on territory
North, while other race men were headed south.
I lit out solo to find, own, and be
My future by strong back, tack, and by mouth;
I knew I'd compete elbow to elbow
With white men, but I still needed a wife
To keep me sane lest I sing a lowbrow
Fool's tune: humming *Hmm, Hmm, hmm* through my life.
Now, I need a few nights of heaven here
To live with a woman, pick out our star.

INT. BASEMENT, NATIONAL PENCIL CO. FACTORY,
MILLEDGEVILLE, GA—
Saturday/Sunday, April 26/27, 1913—DAY

MARY PHAGAN, *thirteen-year-old factory worker, deceased (VO)*

My body's sky; they try to pick a star:
Police ask questions as if, from this far,
I could answer. All I offer lies here.
I'm not resisting or playing coy. Fear
Envelopes the room as much as it filled
My lungs the night all this trouble started.
My eyes look into theirs asking, fighting
To ask, them to keep asking: My sphinxing
Self. If the killer's clues lie between my legs,
I'll act like a cricket, till my body sings.

Photographs speak little of my distrust
Of men: my white slip, knee-high socks. How I
Placed more faith in the father in his eye,
Than all my attempts to avoid men's lust . . .

INT. JAIL—1913—ONE WEEK LATER—NIGHT

LEO FRANK, manager of the National Pencil Company in
Milledgeville, GA, is on trial for the murder of Mary Phagan.
Frank, Jewish, is accused of the crime, but there's no forensic evi-
dence linking him to the murder. But the townspeople and authori-
ties have accused the outsider from Brooklyn, NY. He waits in jail
for another day on trial.

Of the dangers I avoided of lust,
Of frauds against my case, of witnesses
Without a crime, of lies from men unjust—
What can I say? Is there any defense?

Infinite pleadings, naked offerings,
The tenderness of truth reworked, retold—
The truth of childhood is now abhorring—
The Negroes grow pliant, yielding, controlled,

Folding under threats against their own kin,
In workplaces, at home; beaten, breathless,
Under hoods at night, the threat trumps the sin,
And now our fate is weighed by the careless.

To hell with any issues around why;
I just want the past to lie down and die.

EXTERIOR—ON THE ROAD—1913—NIGHT

Believing Leo Frank is innocent, bounty hunter EARL HIGGIN-
BOTTOM travels through the Great Plains in horse and buggy to
Milledgeville, GA, in search of Mary Phagan's true killer.

First, I want the past to lie down and die
While I move ahead and find you: bounty,
Lover, song. I need the whole world to get
Behind me. I need the path to sunset
Lined with prospects not nostalgia. Someday
I'd like to teach myself something new, a
Trade other than binding men, an avenue
To art, to say what I feel, what I knew
Of life. If I can't have love, then no new
Pain can enter these clothes I wear, see?
With no one to lose, no one can lose me.

Like a daguerreotype, my wife lies here,
And her body reminds me she was here,
As the past taunts the present, striking fear.

INT. HOME—MADAME SUL-TE-WAN—1914—DAY

African American actress and contemporary of Lillian Gish,
Madame Sul-Te-Wan appeared in many films for D. W.
Griffith as a maid or mammy figure; she was rarely credited,
not even in *The Birth of a Nation*. She prepares.

Real-life scenes strike fear, while past scenes just taunt,
Watching them on screen. Now, I may stumble
But Madame Sul-Te-Wan will never fall.
The metamorphosis was worth the pain.
The anticipation was worth the wait.
In Louisville, Kentucky, life was calm,
If you wanted to live without living.

I needed more; I decided to change:
The name, the home, but I ain't forgot me.
Griffith gives me a job without credit,
No star to hang a name from. Serving up
A plate of homemade pancakes is my role . . .
No change: I came to play a maid on screen.
It rings clear: Our work on *Birth* brings no love.

INT. HOME, ATLANTA—1915—DAY

Newsreel of D. W. GRIFFITH in his library at home after
the release of his biggest financial success, *The Birth of a Nation*,
which, like Thomas Dixon's *The Clansman* from which it was
adapted, he sees as "An Historical Romance of the Ku Klux
Klan," which was the novel's subtitle.

Birth of a Nation brings a love story
About men and women from bordered soil
During the war, to wide-screen destiny:
The North, it seems, set the country aboil.
While the klieg-lit South tried to end this feud.
This story kept our focus on lovers,
In times when talking about love rang rude.
Look, see how they stare into each other's
Eyes. Pull in. Close-ups bring out emotion,
Brings her moist lips, his tear-filled eyes, their mirth.
They don't want Civil War—just devotion.
Our lovers, like soldiers, rove back and forth.
And when both push passion, pushed to a rest,
Just a touch of sweat slides south, down her breast.

FLASHBACK: EXT.—GREGORY, SD—1904—NIGHT

Front porch of home of Oscar, now homesteading farmer and
Negro novelist. He contemplates his affection for and relationship
with his Scottish neighbor's daughter, AGNES.

Just a hint of sweat, Agnes, on your breast,
Reminds me now of our night in shadow,
Hiding from your father's gaze. He didn't
Know—or care, seems, coming from Scotland—but
Others lie in wait, North and South, to cut
Our throats, but just to think . . . no, I shouldn't
Think of a white woman. This puts me through
A spectrum of scrutiny; a real test

For a race man, a real forecast of pain;
To know our life is hard is no riddle.
This may sound foolish, maybe pivotal,
But Negroes and whites, we're just built for strain.

If we had children, though we'd hope they'd thrive,
Desire builds a war they could not survive.

INT. REV. NEWTON McCRACKEN'S HOME,
CHICAGO—APRIL 21, 1910—DAY

Oscar meets and decides to marry ORLEAN McCRACKEN,
the daughter of a preacher Oscar sees as an after-church-chicken-
dinner-eatin' charlatan. Tensions rise between the father and Oscar.

Rev. Newton McCracken

To survive this war with my girl's husband,
Between this young man and a man like me,
Orlean needs to choose God for her life.

Between him and a Godly man like me,
Well, a young buck loses every time.
She shares my blood, my home, my dreams; he'll see.

You can't tell me nothin'. Love ain't a crime,
Unless it comes outside church. Husband or not:
A husband's gonna lose every time.

Whether he tries to tell me or not,
I've taken care of her and her mother;
No man can tell me what *needs* and what *ought*.

Keep her in church, and stay out of her ear.
You can't break the laws of God, actin' grown.

. . .

Oscar

Man, forget all the laws; we're in love and grown.
Know what's in her prayers, Rev? My hands, my mouth . . .
Look: Preachers' daughters always get their men,
Even when preachers thump Bibles over beds,
Even if the church doesn't say amen;
A preacher's daughter always gets her man.
Like Song of Songs, my left hand holds her head.
Who cares if the church doesn't say amen?
As my right hand embraces her body,
Like Solomon, my left hand holds her head.
And I'll kiss her with the wine of my mouth,
As my right hand embraces her body.
Naked, she comes to me; I'll kiss her mouth
Through the night; like wine, coming, her body.

INT. OFFICE OF GOVERNOR OF GEORGIA—1915—DAY

JOHN M. SLATON, who, after hearing of the trumped-up charges against Leo Frank, and after pressure from liberal groups, decides to commute Frank's sentence down to life in prison, though he believes he was innocent. Slaton believes it's better than giving him a death sentence.

Through the night, unrest breaks. How to survive?
A life worth saving, my conscience to calm . . .
With all on my mind, now, at stake are lives;
Leo Frank's and others lie in the palm

Of my hand, and I have no peace to bring.
That's the problem: Too few consequences
For living wrong. It's now winter, and spring
Is forever coming. Accomplices

To the crime sit on the jury making
Bad decisions, forcing me to play judge.
Georgia is no playground, and tampering
Is beneath my office, but there's a grudge

Growing in the hearts of the townspeople.
Like hands folding into fists, the people.

EXT.—MILLEDGEVILLE—1915—ANONYMOUS—
DAY/NIGHT

African American residents and workers from the National Pencil
Factory of Milledgeville, where the trial is held, and residents of
Marietta, birthplace of Mary Phagan, are threatened by emerging
Klansmen—men calling themselves *The Knights of Mary Phagan*,
emboldened by *The Birth of a Nation*—with the murder of their
families and to burn their homes if they don't bear witness against
Leo Frank.

Like hands folding into fists, the people
Came to find justice, came to blame someone.
When man makes mistakes, work to correct them;
Not a clear lesson for any man's life.
Tough love, dear mirror, barked my reflection,
But now is no time for recollection.
Now, in Milledgeville, I fear for my life.
The factory Negroes, and all of 'em,
Get threats all day and all night by someone,
Who appears as no one, hooded people,

Men with guns. All's I know. And men with guns
Run this trial. Frank is a prisoner
But we're all held hostage, we whom law shuns
Sleep with our shoes on, while saying a prayer.

FLASHBACK: INT.—MICHEAUX HOME, GREGORY, SD—1912—DAY

At the urging of her minister father and her family, his wife, Orlean—after suffering a miscarriage—has left him. Micheaux makes one last effort to make it on his homestead but surrenders on this final day, setting out on a period of itinerancy.

With shoes on feet and prayer on tongue, I drive;
I branch into art from crops with no wife.
Like a face caught off screen, now I'm alive;
I've found my game without wielding a knife.
Though through the lens my eye glints like a knife,
My focus is race to prove I'm alive.
I'm a new Negro; that's how I survive.
Film is my path now, later for a wife.
This ain't one about the dutiful wife,
Or fathers worried their sons won't revive
A South defeated under the North's knife.
This is my work, how I know I'm alive.
This story of a man left by his wife,
Proves a man can choose art over the knife.

•   •   •

I proved man could choose art over the knife
When she asked how much it would cost to make
This "movie thing," what kind of risk involved,
I knew then she would have me plowing fields.

This girl is my past now, not the woman
I once loved. I might be broke but I have
Class, but you can't have class and be cheap. I
Said, "You think Griffith has to deal with this?"
She said, "You ain't Griffith, Negro," as she
Walked out the sod-house door. And I watched as
Her blurred figure burned off the horizon
Faster than my name blew free from her lips.
An apparition in my mind now, but
I still see her . . . though, I must look ahead.

INT. HOTEL ROOM, CHICAGO—JUNE 1913—DAY

Later, midyear, Oscar's loneliness is getting the better of him. He's still trying to make sense of what happened in his marriage, and he's still determined to make it as a writer.

Looking ahead pushes the past deeper
Inside my pocket: memories, jangling
Like loose change but diminishing,
Day in and day out, as I try to figure
Out what comes next. The sky won't predict days
Of prosperity, days of loss, but I
Study. I watch. Take the Epsom Derby:
A woman stepped out in front of the King's
Horse; she was trampled to death. She was a
Suffragist, Emily Davison. Now,
I respect her death, like taking a vow,
She died trying to make change, in her way,
Which baffles the spectators, watching from
The stands. She died to keep from eating crumbs.

        • • •

        Others die complacent, eating crumbs from
        Hands starving them. Most people don't think, see;
        They figure she must've been confused, she
        Must've been trying to take something from
        Or attach something, a flag, to the horse.
        But, no, maybe she just wanted to push

Others to take action, to chart a course
To make others ask why, you know, to flush
Out the rhetoric, the philosophy.
It's hard to find an act more pure than death.
Always appears on the set of our lives
In the background, still, urging us to live—
It's hard to find a message more clear. Death
Comes to spirit us on like family.

. . .

All of the dead ascend to family,
And we take note of our lives, checking in
To see how we're doing with life, what's been
At the center of our hearts. The daily
Jabs at others and their politics seem
Smaller in light of loss, in the wake of
Losing my wife, even this feels extreme—
As if I'm in mourning, though I lost love.
She was with child, double loss, from which there
Was no coming back. Orlean and I knew
Our baby was our last chance to declare
Peace between her father and me. So few
Chances in this world to share a twin bill:
One's love to find, one's calling to fulfill.

. . *

But what else should we try to fulfill? Work
And love. What else is out there? Nothing worth
Pursuing. I've seen men sidetracked by less,
Believing life's a trick, when it's a test
Of will. It's a world filled with temptation.
It's a world of adult situations.
It's up to me to figure out the path,
Whether with a wife or not, the road's wrath
Awaits me. Leaving South Dakota was
A blessing I didn't see because
I couldn't hear the message calling out
For me to stop acting a knockabout.
Where are the voices of expectation?
Of people in action? Their vibration?

. . *

I need the vibration of people in
Action, not those chewing their cud out west,
But the verve of the East Coast: a Brooklyn
Or Harlem, D.C., but no more Midwest
Than Chicago, for sure, but skyscrapers
And crowds, for sure, for sure. I need Negroes
As real race men, not breeders but readers—

And minds adrift like archipelagoes,
Exploring beyond the backs of their hands.
Whenever the sun breaks, peering through clouds,
Swords of light falling through a window, lands
Coming to life—an empty street, a crowd,
Or a field of corn from my past—the strand
Of a story unfolds beneath my hands.

.   .   .

As the story unfolds beneath my hands,
Black stones lift from the ground within my mind,
Not clearing my path, but stones left behind
To show others the way. There are few strands
Of experience to pass on in film.
Those floating around are not sent for me.
Once I get started, I'll clear the debris
From the road; the path gets fired in the kiln.
But I'm getting ahead of myself. I'm
Still learning my way, and, to be fair, white
Men have helped to shape how I see the light
Bend through a doorway for effect, and I'm
Grateful for the gesture, though they did not
Think that I'd ever fully work this knot.

*   *   *

But here I am, working, like it or not,
And a Negro world is building before
Me. If not used, a man's talents dry-rot,
Whether with work or with women, for sure;
If I don't take care of the blessing, I'll
Lose it. Why not take a chance to see what
I can do now with no wife or child while
I only have one mission left, uncut
By lust or love? Even the prophet in
The Valley of Dry Bones could bring to life
Those who once lived. So why should life wear thin
For those who believe but don't have a wife?
Can't wait on love to swing into action.
I look outside, search, find new attractions.

INT. JAILHOUSE, MILLEDGEVILLE, GA—1915—NIGHT

Leo Frank. His last night in jail after the verdict. Later tonight, a group of men calling themselves *The Knights of Mary Phagan* will break him out of jail, drag him to Marietta, and hang him, publicly. He will be the first and only Jewish American, on record, to suffer this horror. Leo thinks about the pain and suffering the trial has caused his wife.

I see you when I look outside, daily,
Even when you're not there. You stand in front
Of me, finding a smile through bad news: I'm
Not coming home. You know I need your smile.
Without freedom to walk through town, I know
You live in prison, too. Yours seems harder
To define than stone, than iron bars; yours
Moves without walls around all corners; yours
Seeks some peace to tamp it down. It's harder
To rake a cup against no bars, you know,
But you find a way to make noise. No smile
Comes when I think of you not smiling. I'm
Left wringing my hands; you keep up the front!
I see you when I look outside, daily.

INT. TRAIN CAR—1917—DAY

Orlean dies from being trampled by a horse on her way to church. After being brought to a whites-only hospital in Chicago, she was refused admittance and died en route to St. Luke's, a hospital that admitted Negroes. Oscar's financial problems have increased after losing the homestead. From his train car, he ruminates on the past few years, embattled with the McCrackens. He begins looking for other ways, including his novels and making films, to not only make a living, but also to make an impact on the public consciousness. In the meantime, he's also trying to deal with loneliness.

Daily, I look outside and I see hell.
You think it's sad? A man with no woman?
Try life as a man with no money. Now
There's a sad story. I can't think sweetheart
When I'm sinking in debt, but, I confess:
Orlean's handwriting was the prettiest
I had ever seen, but film's my wife now.
I left her letters behind to find my-
Self. Screen couples show an Every Man
Loving an Every Woman. I mold
Stand-ins for us, sculptures looking the part,
But, being an artist in need of love,
My hammer shattered us like a sculpture.
Dear Orlean, this is our story to tell.

MONTAGE: INT./EXT. MOVIE HOUSES—NIGHT—
MILLEDGEVILLE . . . MARIETTA . . . CLEVELAND . . .
CHICAGO . . . KANSAS CITY . . . MOBILE . . . LITTLE
ROCK . . . AND MANY MORE—1915—ANONYMOUS

African Americans all over America go to the movies, as they have
since before the Lincoln Picture Company started releasing "race
films" in 1913. But they must deal with Jim Crow laws and sit in
"Nigger Heaven," the balcony.

Men and women have some stories to tell.
Most men and women have stories to tell.
Life be pourin' out 'em, like trains skippin' off rails.

Movies tell stories I wish I could live.
Heroes say what I can't, but *still* get to live.
But I'd play the villain, given one chance to live.

I go to movies by foot, bus, or train.
I get across town by foot, bus, or train.
Man, all kinds of travel, brakes one helluva strain.

When the hero wants to sleep with a girl,
He'll deep-sea dive just to find her a pearl.
Whatever it takes, he says, to sleep with the girl.

At the movies, my arm falls over her shoulder.
At the movies, we keep our minds on each other.

INT.—GEORGIA—1915—NIGHT

Earl Higginbottom, on the trail of JIM CONLEY, whom he
believes to be Phagan's killer, has arrived in the state of Georgia.
His first night there, like every night alone, brings his mind to his
deceased wife, HATTIE. He decides to go to a movie to clear
his head.

Even at a movie, I keep my mind
On my wife. I forget war, focus on
What I loved before talk of secession:
Hattie, my wife, is all my head can find.

If hands hold memories, mine remember her
Feet soaking in water basins: my hands
Dry her toes. I surrender: her finger
Parts my hair when she oils my scalp. Man's
Every morning dims to less certain
With every night's regret. I see vestiges
Of battlefields, fallen soldiers, women
Of whose fates I dare not speak, shortages

Of food, of work, and, still, men want to fight;
Like mine, their shadows cast from fallen light.

INT. NEW YORK PENN STATION—AUGUST 18, 1915—
DAY, 6 A.M.

The Crescent Star enters New York's Penn Station from Atlanta,
transporting the body of Leo Frank. The *New York Times* reports
a "Negro sophisticate" was in the crowd . . . Oscar.

Their shadows are cast from the light falling
Through the windows, the way shadows crawl and
Float, all at once. The windows resist and
Aid the gaze of crowds more than sun streaming

Through, but the shadows persist against light
Setting, as if awaiting an actor
To come forward, hit his mark. An actor,
However, would enjoy life in the light.

Leo Frank has no voice to play his role,
To move from the shadows. Who plays his role?
The body is already at rest. What
More can a corpse do beyond continue

As totem? What can a memory do?
The body is already at rest. What?

INT. HARLEM HOTEL ROOM—AUGUST 18, 1915—NIGHT

Oscar was in Georgia and sat in on the *Frank v. State* trial. He
believes Griffith's *The Birth of a Nation*, released to success just
before the verdict, had influence on these events. He tells others
his opinion.

Their bodies already lie at rest. What,
If anything, could Leo Frank and
Mary Phagan do to any man? And
I mean dead or alive. I'm asking what

Does a mob think happens if a man is
Jew or Negro in a community
Of white? I can't change a community,
But seek dignity, capital; life is

Changing daily. Film has great influence,
Maybe more than money itself. I need
To stop farming, start sowing film. I need
To stop dreaming, start having influence

On lives, not just Negroes but on whites, too.
Like taxes, we all pay when death comes due.

INT. OFFICES OF LINCOLN FILM COMPANY, LOS
ANGELES—1918—DAY

NOBLE JOHNSON, cofounder of the Lincoln Film Company
with his brother George, agrees to work with Oscar to help distrib-
ute and promote his films. The deal falls through, though. Oscar
goes on to make and distribute his own film under the Micheaux
Film and Book Company out of Sioux City.

Listen, after these new taxes are paid,
After the snow melts over the country,
After the parties, after the rent gets paid,
After, for once, we feel like one country,

After the crops are picked and meted out,
I want people to see our lives as lives,
Not sharecroppers, not rations or handouts,
Not stumps to serve, but as heroes—real lives.

So open the main floor to Negroes. Yes,
Open the curtain and reveal the screen.
I want them to laugh, cry, quarrel, and, yes,
Make love after seeing our films on screen.

You can live like a saint but have nothing.
Why not raise hell? What's to be lost? . . . Nothing.

EXT. CHURCH STEPS, MARIETTA—1918—DAY

Jim Conley, three years later and many years after that, is constantly questioned about the Leo Frank v. Mary Phagan trial.

I knowed hell and I had nothin' to lose,
But I been tellin' 'em I had nothin'
To do with no Mary Phagan; now, I
Told the courts I helped Mr. Frank with her,
But I *had* to say, what they said to say.
That's jus' how it goes: Me or him. The world
Ain't studyin' ole Jim Conley; the world
Care about the girl 'cause she white; all they say
Is our children ain't safe, meaning like her,
Young white girls. Man, they ain't talking 'bout my
Children. They threatens to kill mines. Nothin'
Left to give; I got nothin' left to lose.

Say, what you will, 'bout my story changin',
I sleeps in peace, and thas not just dreamin'.

INSERT SHOT: THE *CHICAGO DEFENDER*, HEADLINE:
Woman Raped and Lynched by Mob of Southern White Men,
December 18, 1919

CORDELLA and ARCH STEVENSON are attacked in their
sleep after a white farmer accuses their son of setting fire to his
barn. Their son had not been to town for months.

To slumber Wednesday night, at peace, dreaming;
To wake to men invading their cabin,
Breaking down the door, knocking first to fool
Cordella and Arch to think they had guests;
To barge in, hooded, armed, and looking (they
Say) for her "no 'count" son, finding her there
In bedclothes, husband Arch, in his long johns,
Shotguns now to his head, he runs to town
For help. No law man, no race man aided
Him. Cordella, stripped naked, dragged out
To Mobile & Ohio Railroad tracks,
"Maltreated," evidence of men left on
Her body, her body left there hanging
By hands unknown until Friday morning.

FLASHBACK: INT. ATLANTA HOTEL ROOM—
1915—DAY

Oscar reads the verdict for and sentencing of Leo Frank. He is disturbed by the Negro "witnesses" who testified against Frank. He sees them as traitors not just to their race, but also to race relations with Jews. This sticks with him as he begins to write and to think about film.

Bootblacks. Scared maids. Unknown hands on Sunday
Mornings in churchgoers' pockets. I tire
Of ignorant Negroes and hate their fears
More, some days, than the whites threatening them.
The act of lynching Frank, reading Monday
Morning how "race men" witnessed against fire
Threats, makes me wonder: Don't they own guns? Years
Of threats, lynchings, and rape, and torn from limb

To limb, and they can't see one tree leads to
Another? What did they expect? To start
Living free? Griffith set us back 50
Years, and these witnesses also played roles.
Meaning they need hero roles to witness.
Set clocks 50 years ahead, starting now.

MONTAGE: INT. OSCAR MICHEAUX'S MIND—1915–1918— DAY/NIGHT

Growing tired of the emboldened responses to Griffith's *The Birth of a Nation* and the violence in the wake of the Leo Frank trial, Oscar realizes he needs a new medium to reach the public: film. He sees the effect film has on the psyche and behavior of people, so he embarks on a quest to learn this new art form. He begins by deciding to adapt his roman à clef, *The Homesteader*, to the screen.

Starting now, focused, I see through a lens
All the life I've blurred in my head, chambers
Underground in my mind, I now explore.
When two figures come together to share
Space, find a way to frame their bodies to
Express the love or distance between them . . .
To compose the movement of a woman
Taking stairs, presents a problem: Women,
In motion, show graceful intent. For them,
Walking is art, yes, crossing their legs, too,
While sitting, reading a book, is art. Share
This space with a man, and now you explore
A whole new problem: Loading this chamber,
With both, challenges and sharpens the lens.

. . .

Sharpen the focus in your lens, and you
Sharpen your view of the world; you can see
How people inhabit space in their lives,
How the skin of Negroes and whites both play
With light, how both reflect from within—light.
How often does one stop to notice this
In the course of one's day? How often do
We think of what our shadows and light do
Together in a space in the world? This
Alone would slow down a day, watching light.
This alone would invite one out to play.
This alone would allow, into your life,
Others. But, no, in life one rarely sees
How light bounces off someone back to you.

. . .

As the light bounces back and as the shot
Composes the light and as the gesture
From the actor's hand moves and as rain
Falls on the set fortuitously, saving
A day when we thought we'd have to create
Our own storm, and as we come to understand
How all these elements work, we learn to make

Film. We learn to adapt to the things we make.
Any farmer can tell you, *Understand*
The land and you'll sow. But film can create
The land, the mood of the sky, it can save
The union; if need be, it brings the rain,
It brings sun, it brings both in one gesture,
If need be. It brings life in just one shot.

. . .

In just one shot, I could offer a kiss
From a man crossing a room from the left
Of the screen, which offers ease on the eyes
As opposed to his crossing from the right
Or from the bottom up into the frame.
I never thought about how important
The line of vision was in one's daily
Routine. I walk outside and stare daily.
First, I look at the feet, and the import
Of this comes from understanding the frame:
You can create character with the right
Shoes, a woman's arched foot—both draw eyes;
Start there and she's sexy. There's little left
To say. Pull in for the close-up, the kiss.

Pull in. Time for the close-up: the money.
People give to film like no other art
Or charity I've seen. I imagine
It's for selfish reasons: Everyone wants
Their name in lights, their hand in making
Some howling beautiful thing, the power
To bring women to tears and men to knees
With a flash of powder, a face framed, a knee
Exposed from beneath a dress. The power
Of film, the love of the public, to make
The public love you, feeds the many wants
Of others and offers love back. Image
After image comes down to bringing art
To those in need. And I need their money.

I need money to get started. Novels
Call for sweat and some imagination.
Finding time to write was the biggest block,
But film calls for cash and bodies to work
With me. I like having workers and I
Like having money, so this just suits me
Fine. And I'll give them quality, too. Film

Costs too much to make any junk. My film
Needs to show all sides of the Negro. My
Idea for the screen needs to inspire. I'm
The man I've never seen on screen: I work,
I think, I create, I love. There's no block
Of wood we're carved from. Imagination
Can't cast me on screen. I'm old. I'm novel.

      • • •

I'll cast characters from *The Homesteader,*
And offer the public a new Negro
To consider. No more blackface Sambos;
No more mammies without lives, without homes
Of their own. Who wants to see, all at once,
As if asleep, a woman or man act
As if their souls were out of work and their
Bodies were just hired? This ghost of theirs
Dies on screen at my hand. People will act
Like people whose souls you can knock on, once
I get the camera. The setting? A home
Or field, classroom or bedroom—no Sambos
Or mammies allowed. Just real-life Negroes,
Starting now, on screen, a real homesteader.

INSERT SHOT: THE *CHICAGO DEFENDER*, REVIEW:
THE HOMESTEADER:
Oscar Micheaux's Famous Story Makes Great Film, February 22, 1919

Starting now, the film we've all been waiting
With held breath to see. *The Homesteader*, film
By Oscar Micheaux. The film debuted at
Eighth Colored Regiment Armory at
8 P.M., 35th and Forest Streets,
Chicago. Film of marriage and deceit,
Film on which he bet the farm, literally;
Film against church, against hate, against lust
And fate; film of bootstraps and pulling, back-
Bones and standing upright; film with lines wrapped
Around the block; film in eight reels, first for
Race films; a film so good, tickets sold for
10 cents more; a film with the word "nigga,"
But used, this time, by us on screen with hugs.

CUT TO: EXT. MAIN ST., MILLEDGEVILLE—1919—DAY

Earl Higginbottom catches up with Jim Conley. Thinking he will
bring the man to confess, he soon realizes Conley is a lost cause and
probably not only not smart enough to have gotten away with the
crime, but also that Conley is living an imprisonment of sorts, any-
way. Earl sees Conley as a bad vaudeville act in blackface, except
Conley is real.

Used to a life without hugs, not even
From his own kind, Conley is the saddest
Negro I've ever met born in freedom.
Made *me* feel like a man without freedom.
The Phrenologist Coon seemed the saddest
Amos & Andy skit I'd seen, even
Though they wrote it, but now I live it,
Talking to this Negro. I can tell *What's*
In his head by what's in his pocket: no—
Thing. He's empty. A glass to fill up. No,
He lives emptied out; he's to live out what
They want. Unlike him, as a boy, dammit,
I was a man. But I stood up when held
Down; though, when on hard times, I still was held.

INT./EXT.—1919

Spirit of Mary Phagan, thirteen-year-old factory worker. (VO)

Mama says you have to fall on hard times
To know how to live; she says I don't know
How hard life bears down on adults, "Damn near
Will kill ya just to live," she says. No doubt,
Mama. I lie in evidence of truth.
I believe her sayings now, but I can't
Trust the John Keats poem from my lessons:
"A thing of beauty is a joy for ever . . ."; I
Would believe Mr. Keats, but I think he
Died three years after he wrote the poem?
So fo . . . fo . . . "For ever?" my voice stutters.
You see, I don't exist; youth is fleeting,
More a puzzle than "a joy," Mr. Keats.
I ponder your poem even in death . . .

INT./EXT.—1951

Spirit of Oscar Micheaux. After a long career as one of the most
successful independent filmmakers of all time, thirty-eight films
from 1919 to 1948, Oscar dies March 25, 1951, of a heart attack
while on a business trip in Charlotte, NC. His body is interred in
Great Bend, KS. (VO)

Even in death—Hollywood's star-lined streets,
Emblazoned with money and all green lights,
With handshakes and the smiles and the gold streets
Of studios spotlit and the dim lights
Of front offices—I'd make films in streets.
I'm free: My life was always dreamed in lights;
And now, I've shared ideas in many streets;
As you walk them, watch my labor through light.

What more can I make of a well-wrought life?
As Yeats said, "I spread my dreams under your feet."
And maybe one day, I will have a star
On Hollywood Blvd., and the star
Will hold my dream, which will lie at your feet
At night, my lonely gift, my work, my life . . .

EXT.—CHICAGO—FEBRUARY 20, 1919—NIGHT

Earl Higginbottom, having given up the bounty-hunting trade, moves to Chicago to work in the steel mills. Tonight, he attends the premiere of *The Homesteader*. (VO)

Night: In a city under the North Star,
He stops. He's both in delight and dismay,
To watch not a single painted blackface,
The face he faced with horror on his own.

All he knew is now history. Ticket
Stubs sit in hands of the Negro patrons:
Proof of collaboration never seen
Firsthand, between a race man and a dream.

What a surprise! A film by a Pullman!
And scenes, never seen, come in an array
Of voices, lighting a path to a seat
Like ushers to a future, lighting a
City with farmers wearing spit-shined shoes;
Farmers from Midwest farms travel by train;

．　．　．

By train the bent-back sharecroppers come, too.
They come to Chicago to see, on screen,
Themselves in a different light, no dis-
Grace, just the scent of hard work wafting to
Release in the projector's glow, the glow
Releasing some maids, drivers, and bootblacks;

Small songs of faith from bounty hunters' hearts,
The quiet songs heard only in the bed-
Room at the end of a long trail. Tonight
The music made on farms will rise up from
Streets: Detroit, Cleveland, Kansas City, and
Cities alike. Who knows from where our next
Hero hails, but know tonight patrons sit
Silently—not to show you to your seats.

FADE OUT

III

Do the Right Thing

(Spike Lee, 1989)

The days were a skillet on a red-hot eye of a stove.
The men on the corner, the couple in their apartment,
the kids playing under a fire hydrant's relief
were all sitting, loving, or playing in a skillet.

Heat rose off the assonance of summer language.
Some called it music; others called it fire.
The days were a skillet but the nights were a match
lighting the gas. No moon appeared, only steam

rising off the sidewalks from the day. Feet
danced on the skillet, and smoke alarms sounded.
Moths, fierce as kids at play on a summer day, burst
from musty closets. People were evicted,

put out like butter sliding across a skillet's face.
Most of us were outside by then, swatting bees,
swatting flies; we outlived the life span
of giraffes and cheetahs, made for this weather,

or we sat on our stoops, indolent but defiant,
simply escaping the drama of our own lives.
Even those indoors without air-conditioning—
we like to believe, at least—escaped the heat

somehow. Mookie, to cool her fire, melted
ice cubes on Tina's nipples.

Radio Raheem stole ink off
Robert Mitchum's knuckles. He took the heat,

too, casting *LOVE* and *HATE* into digital bling.
When did "soul brother" become an anachronism
too hot for air-conditioned conversation? In Sal's
Pizzeria, Buggin Out bugs:

"Sal, why ain't no brothers up on your wall?"
Smiley, auguring smoke before nightfall,
carried matches. The day is a skillet on a red-hot eye
of a stove; later, a cop has Radio Raheem

in a choke hold. Later we will light candles
for Radio Raheem. If a man takes a baseball bat
to another man's property, that's a skillet, too.
If a man throws a barrel through a plate glass window,

others will follow. A pyrrhic victory is a pyre of life
possessions set ablaze to save lives. Catharsis is the moth's
flight toward the flame, fluttering in the spotlight, or
first fluttering then fighting the power

to flutter, but consumed by the heat until all we know
of its shimmer is how one smolders to survive.

Run Lola Run

(Tom Tykwer, 1999)

The same questions come and the same answers
lead to more questions, and so it goes, on and on,
the sea's tide—all are questions, all are answers.

Does Manni, who waits in fear, suffer alone
or does Lola, who tries to find him,
suffer more, trying to solve his problem, one

solution after another? Why find money for him
who lost what he did not own in the first place?
Perhaps paradise will look like this for them:

He will wait, and she will arrive to kiss his face,
solving his dilemma, and they will begin again;
she won't grow tired, and he won't join the chase

to figure things out for himself. Again
she will know what to do when all is lost.
Repeating her mistakes won't be insane—

for once. Acting for love at any cost
will be brilliant, even in death;
and the two will have what most

wish for in life: A last laugh as their final breath.
In full complicity, they'll see
the sleepwalking of Lady Macbeth

as a waste of time; no guilt should be
a part of their night. Why shouldn't they share
this dream between them? Free

of the pain of the day? And where
else could they put this need? Does
the lover who dies in your dreams stay there?

Will you mourn when you awaken? The buzz
of the alarm signals opportunity, but
why awaken only to grow apart again? Does

the game repeat itself with a hit to the gut?
The longing despite resisting . . . both are tough,
especially when the clock ticks for a couple, but

facing these dangers again seems enough.
We ask, Don't they get tired of fighting,
of repeating their crises? Maybe they're calling our bluff.

Maybe the rhythm of the day breaking
over them is enough to change our reviews
of a couple making big mistakes, but forgiving?

No couple trying says, *We don't have issues*;
it's the *not* trying that more couples need to eschew.

I've Heard the Mermaids Singing

(Patricia Rozema, 1987)

Often, I find myself in situations
for which there are no adequate epigraphs.
My days fill with temp work,
part-time, and I'm in another office,
the next day, day after day,
as a Girl Friday . . . or a *Person* Friday, now—
though life hasn't changed
with the title—the same world
unfolding around me: Women
with babies, couples in love,
women on bicycles or swimming,
women of all kinds, but none
who look like me. My lens sees
through them; I send my gaze like a song,
but they don't sing back. I notice
some, like Gabrielle, for instance,
from whom I cannot take my eyes
back; I fall in love with her, the way
most art lovers fall for a Matisse.
You cherish a Matisse, but you don't
want to kiss or hug one. But, what's
so wrong with imagining the Matisse
wanting to kiss me back, seeing into me?

Let's say the Matisse is a woman,
looking so deeply into my core till
it looks like a tower to climb on a sunny day,
and the wind begins blowing
the closer she gets to the top, and birds
fly around the top stairs of the tower,
but she grows tired of climbing.
The closer she gets to the top,
she can see all the colors comprising me,
and she thinks, *Maybe I can't make it*
to the top of her tower, maybe even a Matisse
isn't good enough to reach such beauty.
She says this as she feels the light
on her face . . . And I tell her,
Fear not the height, the distance of the fall . . .
Keep your eyes on the point
of ascent; yes, the clouds swell heavy,
the rain comes hard, the legs grow weary.
Ah, but the gasp for air . . . Ah, but the view . . .

Black Girl

(Ousmane Sembène, 1966)

I listened to the palavering: Birds with car horns
as the sun went down. Once I began

to understand their conversations, I started my days
by eavesdropping like a citizen of privilege

and apathy. Antibes reminds me
of Dakar the way a new lover brings

to mind the mistakes I made with the one before.
As I pass other women in the marketplace,

home is soon clouded in memory
by the air of authority festering

behind sunglasses, amid cigarette smoke.
All faces look alike and no face reminds me

of anyone I knew from another life.
Yesterday, I was introduced as "our girl,"

a possessive I've never felt in my country.
The gift I offer now is a face behind a mask,

a mask of a face to haunt them
long after mine fades away behind it.

Dear young couple, you
who hired me to look after your young,

give up on the roman à clef in which you
imagined me as a nameless character.

Give up on subterfuge to control
the woman you imagined me to embody.

My body, lifeless, politically still,
still has a chance to rustle a few trees

inside your aristocratic heads.

American Gigolo

(Paul Schrader, 1980)

The shirts folded; the ties rolled;
the suits hung in descending,
monochromatic earth tones; shoes
horned and shined; and the selection of the right
combination choreographed to a
not-quite jazz but a jazz-inflected voice,
nonetheless, pouring from Bang & Olufsen speakers,
bouncing off high ceilings in a condo,
minimally but well appointed: Here is a space
in which a man can make bad decisions.

He's Julian, the gigolo, and to a teenage boy
sitting in a movie theater in 1980,
he looms large as a Sphinx
in front of a Vegas hotel;
he looks like the answer to the riddle
of what it means to be a man.
If you follow Julian, who is framed for murder,
set up by someone he once called on
in the middle of the night as a friend,

you can trace his steps back to salvation.
Cut to: Julian crossing the hotel bar to a booth
in back where a woman, Michelle, sits.
Though she's the woman who will save him,
and the only prop separating them

is a table with cocktails and appetizers,
his presence interferes. The wall between them
should blow over with a whisper in her ear,
but like most of us, Julian can't see the one

who loves him. Though she's already been found,
he keeps searching, distracted by bodies
floating in his wake. Like most of us,
he gives up, believing
there's nothing left to believe in.
Perhaps his nonbelief makes him a hero,
perhaps without insecurity he seems
less believable as a man. Without his mistakes,
we'd have no story. Without his nights

to pass through we'd be less intrigued. Perhaps
he believed his naked body could be a torch
lighting a path for a lover he thought
was waiting just up ahead. Cut to:
Two hours later, a lifetime in film hours,
Julian is in jail now
speaking through a Plexiglas wall,
when he asks Michelle, "Why has it taken so long
for you to come to me?" All Michelle can do

is shake her head and smile.
She knows she never left him,
never needed his pleas to bring her back;
she never needed his wounds or his prison sentence
to heal him or to break him free.
When there is no more ground to search,
when the sun goes down, he turns
around, tracing his steps back to his
beginning, the night in the hotel bar,

the morning after in his bed; he
allows himself to go back there,
where she had always been.
How she covered his tracks with kisses . . .
How she stood through all his rages and his accusations . . .
He needed to ask questions whose answers
he finally found in simply walking out
of the prison he built for himself,
in the love we think we must earn through suffering.

Blazing Saddles

(Mel Brooks, 1975)

What's so funny about racism
is how the racists never get the joke.
In most settings, racists stick out
like Count Basie's Orchestra in the middle
of a prairie, just as awkward as he is

elegant compared to the world around him.
And, if you still don't get it, imagine
a chain gang with perfect pitch
singing Cole Porter's "I Get a Kick Out of You"
to their overseer, whose frustration swells so

for an "authentic-nigger work song,"
he and his crew demonstrate their darkest
desires and break into song themselves,
"De Camptown ladies sing this song,
Doo-da, doo-da," kicking up their heels

in the dirt, tasting an old slave
trick on their tongues, each syllable
falling from their lips like a boll
of cotton. Funny, to the naked eye,
but consider the Native American

who speaks Yiddish, emerging from the dust
of the Old West, reminding us
of how we learn to comfort in making

ourselves a little uncomfortable
over time in the fossils of race.

Jump cut: Black Bart, our hero, enters
town where danger awaits
him, our hero, who we hope
to see beat up bad guys
and win the woman, even when

the hero is black and the woman,
Lili von Shtupp, is German. *One false move
and the nigger gets it.* Yes, self-sacrifice
holding his gun to his own head,
but the unwitting white liberals save him

from himself, which is their lives' mission.
You see, what's so funny about racists
is how they never get the joke,
because the joke always carries some truth.
Notice how we can laugh in recognizing

a Sambo of our own design—
in our own likeness, a likeness we own—
so we can laugh at the absurd pain of it all.
This joke, like aloe smoothed on a wound,
like a black man trying to do a job

in a town where he's not wanted,
like a black man unzipping his pants
in the Old West for a white woman in a hotel
room in the center of this town. Did I mention
how he was just released from a chain gang?

Did I mention that she was an exotic dancer
who slept with men for money, helping them
hang their insecurities on a hook
on the back of a hotel-room door before entering?
Careful with your laughter; one false move and

Nigger here gets appropriated. That's not funny
to you? Well, when they saw themselves
on screen in their comedy-drama romance,
in the theater's darkness, they laughed.
They needed to see it projected

on the wide screen to get a good cathartic laugh
from the tragedy of the 20th century.
And it's okay to laugh at these ironies
today because they're blown from a wind
of past pain, with the velocity of memory.

You see, when the Jewish artist has suffered
enough, he knows he can strike back
with just a stroke of laughter: A black man *shtupping*
a German floozy, who tries to ensnare him
between her legs, but gets hoisted by her own

garter petard? Well, that's just some funny *scheiße*.
So, please, excuse all this humor
wrapped in truth—or its chiasmus—
ready or not, stand back, please,
and back away from all those stereotypes

restraining you from stereotypes you
aspire to. As you deny self
through elective surgery on your nose or lips,
excuse me, please, as I rear back in laughter;
and, excuse me, as I recall the 1970s

and remember myself laughing
blue-black gut-bursting songs of truth. Yeah,
please excuse me, folks, as I whip this out.

Westworld

(Michael Crichton, 1973)

I escaped from *Westworld*, the amusement park for adults,
or maybe it never existed; though I do remember a vivid
weekend there, and shooting a man, like in the song,

just to see how it felt, which is kinda how the brochure
pitched the experience—"replicate a *High Noon* shoot-out,
and spend a night in an Old West brothel"—and I couldn't say no:

An artificial time in an out-of-focus place in my memory . . .
I shot a man once . . . Maybe I have not lived my dreams.
Some people actually like the idea of paying for sin

up front, a fee so they can feel free
of the guilt and consequence of actually
paying for their sins later. Like sleeping with a stranger

one sunny Wednesday afternoon as lambent light,
like a cry, first rising, then, once subdued,
falling over their bodies through a sheer curtain . . .

You think, No consequence to a time and place
edited from the context of your daily life;
this time, this place, doesn't really count.

Maybe in my dreams, I get to taste all
of my fetishes in this life twice and then some,
and I have flashbacks at the most inappropriate moments . . .

Maybe this is why I enter this world away from my own.
Once I accept this as a perfectly legal way to dream, a girl
wearing hot pants: She runs with lamps to light a corner

of the room, just a façade, at the end
of a street, in a wood-planked town opening
between the thumbs of a director,

who motions to motionless actors,
standing inside a saloon, waiting for characters to fill,
till Action! is yelled to them, and town folk

turn on their marks: Cowboys burn into frame:
Yul Brynner, the robot gunslinger, grows confidence;
the Madame earns her name;

Derby hats, strands of pearls,
stockings with a hint of garter,
pockets with swatches of hankie,

waxed mustaches, arched eyebrows,
and the camera, the camera repeats
the eye's questions of what is acting and what is life.

Zephyrs blow across the set, either from the west
or from a man strong enough to support its whirling fronds.
The set is hot when Yul, the gunslinger in the black hat,

says a line to make the heroine in petticoats swoon,
as I throw my white hat in the dirt. I'm pissed:
I paid $1,000 a day for this, and I still don't get the girl?

Beneath the black hat, the gunslinger's mechanical blue eyes
squint in my direction. My hand is on my gun hip,
but something goes wrong; Yul is off script.

And off camera, a shot fires,
and so the camera follows the smoke,
the smoke from the sighing gun.

And there stands Yul with skin hanging
from his steel skull; he shot me in the shoulder,
but not before I put out his eye.

Perhaps none of this happened, but running
past tumbleweeds with the half-Yul-Brynner-half-robot
gunslinger in pursuit, felt real enough to cast as memory.

Maybe I remember sins I didn't pay for in advance,
in which I wore the black hat, as I chased a man,
who ran for his life from my rattling body,

pursuing him straight off the set into reality,
where we stood in the middle of a street—
maybe we fought over his wife; hell, maybe I just owed

the man money—but we did face each other, squinting,
drawing our guns to decide our fates, and yes, there was smoke.

The Cabinet of Dr. Caligari

(Robert Wiene, 1920)

Streets anesthetized in neon lights,
I walk through them in sleep,
deep in sleep, as an excuse

for acts I might only dream
of committing while wide awake.
What if I see you and call your name

in this state of being? What if I take your hand?
Well, I won't be held responsible for what happens
in shadows, so don't even ask:

Nothing comes to light when I'm awake.
You stepped behind the curtain to see
The Somnambulist, at your own

risk. By daylight, we sleepers are not allowed
to follow the dictates of our hearts.
Through the dark woods, one of you

asked me to assume my identity of sleepwalker.
You put me to bed, and, on command,
you woke me up to divert suspicion

from your name. But the mystery soon
solves itself. You will come to me
when the sun reaches its peak, offering details

of the night before, asking me to confirm your dream
as reality, and you will see me for who I really am,
The Great Caligari, a legend to some

but a dream to others, and, for your own sanity,
I will restrain you; at last, you will know your cure.

Ikiru

(Akira Kurosawa, 1952)

Upon hearing news of death approaching,
he sits and sings under the pulse of falling snow.
He doesn't think of papers stacked on his desk
at his government job, the view through a window
of a wall; the presence of no one listening
to pleas from citizens; the eight-hour-workday
eyes through which the citizens glare to fill out forms;
snowflakes building on the windowsill
with the patience of government workers;
the workers without the snow's patience,
refusing to help the citizens they serve. Today,
he examines the story of his life, which is to say,
he accepts any mistakes he's made, refusing
any excuses for himself. He remembers, just yesterday
he woke eager to attack his To-Do List of mistakes.
It's the news he read on the doctor's face, this news
brought him to act so beautifully today. It's just now
that all the words the world tried to say, make so much sense,
now when the face on the clock looks at him with such pity.
He forces a smile, tries to make the seconds hand trip a bit.
For years, he'd thought himself too old to learn
new tricks, to master a hand of cards or a woman's heart.
A man must be willing to look like a child,
who has yet to believe in death,
to attain his desires. Yet he believed
if he kept repeating what he would never master—

making love, making money, making happiness—if,
through the failures, he kept nodding his head,
he thought this would make him appear mature.
Once when he was a child, drowning in a pond, he had a chance
to decipher the mystery of living. As he drowned,
he kept grasping at the mystery, but there was nothing to hold;
suddenly, he gave up fighting,
giving himself over to water, and he popped to the top,
floating, believing he had pulled himself to the surface.
But surviving is not the same as living, is it? Suddenly, he wants
to buy a hat, cock the brim to the side. Why not buy a young woman
silk stockings, which she'll only wear to his funeral?
Why not clear off his desk, push a form through the system
to build a playground with a swing for which he's too old
to enjoy? His dilemma is either an opportunity or a
final prayer, and he realizes there's no choice there at all.
Why not sit on the swing under falling snow
and sing a song about the brevity of life
for the children making footprints behind him,
though the footprints will melt with the morning sun?

The Red Balloon

(Albert Lamorisse, 1956)

Tribes of boys are jealous of the one
tethered to the red balloon. Adults
don't seem to understand him either.

See, the boy runs with his balloon
trailing behind him; even when he
opens his grip, the balloon obeys

and, as if it had legs, runs
alongside him. Can you see?
Even in the silences between them,

even when the boy is not there,
even when the boy cannot come
to play, the balloon—the boy's

secret, this one boy's one friend—
remains loyal, rising and falling
right along with the boy.

The balloon keeps returning,
around every corner, down every alleyway,
and as more of its fidelity reveals,

the other boys try to destroy its élan,
but the balloon simply gathers more
balloons, and something common to this boy

appears fantastic to others: He gathers
the strings attached to the balloon
bouquet. He takes flight over the city,

until he's even more of a mystery
in the squinting eyes of the boys,
the boys looking into the sun,

which gleams like a future too bright
to look into. The boys
wield slingshots to bring him

back down to the soil, the soil
which does not stir beneath their shoes
like the clouds do beneath his

as he continues to float beyond
their skinned-kneed jealousies,
as the rectrices of his feet

steer clear of their stones.

And then their mouths hang agape.

And then there is no hope; his floating away,

his act of no-act-at-all for him, is already
too many octaves above their voices.

One Week

(Buster Keaton, 1920)

Buster Keaton's every move strikes
without the sting of pity, just the sweat
of arms swinging hammers and nailing
planks of wood; he builds a scene to astonish
all in awe. There's nothing more physical
than a man in love, but jealousy
renders me still: The story opens
with him marrying my ex. At first,
I simply want to warn him, but they seem
so happy . . . Simply put, he appears
to have it all: A young bride, a home
as a wedding gift, and a plot of land.
What else am I to do but foil his plans?
The home comes with directions in eight
sequentially numbered boxes marked
Portable House Co. All he has
to do is follow the order and build;
then the couple will be complete. But
will he make it all work? Well, the blur
of their happiness overcomes me,
so I switch the numbers on the boxes.
And, yes, Buster constructs a catastrophe,
but he builds this mechanical mess
with his calloused hands, which is enough
to impress his bride. I can say, at least,
I tried. At least I built a ravishing

quandary for him to solve with her
as witness, and they'll always have me
to thank for the memory of how far
they came together, while cleaning up
my muddle. And, still, I crave the problems
and the rigors of solving them, day
after day, the weeklong, filled with the charms
of young love, arm in arm without script,
without compass, walking anew into
a set constructed from life's dilemmas.

Oldboy

(Park Chan-Wook, 2003)

If one rainy night you find yourself
leaving a phone booth, and you meet a man
with a lavender umbrella, resist
your desire to follow him, to seek
shelter from the night in his solace.
Later, don't fall victim to the Hypnotist's
narcotic of clarity, which proves
a curare for the heart; her salve
is merely a bandage, under which memories
pulse. Resist the taste for something still
alive for your first meal; resist the craving
for a touch of a hand from your past.
We live some memories,
and some memories are planted. There's
only so much space for the truth
and the fabrications to spread out
in one's mind. When there's no more
space, we grow desperate. You'll ask
if practicing love for years in your mind,
prepares you for the moment.
If practicing to defend one's life
is the same as living? You'll
hole up, captive, in a hotel room
for fifteen years and learn to find
a man within you, which will prove
a painful introduction to the trance

into which you were born. Better
to stay under the spell of your guilt,
than to forget; you've already released
your pain onto the world; don't believe
there's some joy in forgetting.
There's no joy in the struggle to forget.
And what appears as an endless verdant field
only spreads across a building's rooftop;
your peaceful sleep could be a fetal position,
which secures you in a suitcase in this field.
A bell rings, and you fall out of this luggage
like clothes you no longer fit. Now what to do?
You remember when you were the man
who fit those clothes, but you've forgotten this
world. Even forgotten scenes from your life,
leave shadows of the memory,
haunting your spirit
until, within a moment's glance,
strangers passing you on the street,
observe history in your eyes. Experience
lingers through acts of forgetting,
small acts of love or trauma
falling from the same place. Whether
memory comes in the form of a stone
or a grain of sand, they both sink in water.
A tongue—even if it were, say, sworn

to secrecy; or if it were cut from one's mouth;
yes, even without a mouth to envelop
its truth—the tongue continues to confess.

ACKNOWLEDGMENTS

Grateful acknowledgment to the editors of the following publications in which these poems, sometimes in different forms, originally appeared:

Black Renaissance/Noire: from "The Homesteader": *Hotel Room, Chicago*; *Jim Conley*; *Earl Higginbottom*

Boston Review: "Metropolis, restored edition"

Callaloo: from "The Homesteader": *Birth of a Nation, Flashback Micheaux, Micheaux at Home*; "Killer of Sheep," "M," "Rififi," "The Brother from Another Planet," "The Red Shoes"

The Collagist: "Nosferatu," "The Great Train Robbery," "The Cabinet of Dr. Caligari"

Fusion: "American Gigolo," "I've Heard the Mermaids Singing," "Last Year at Marienbad," "The Mack," "Oldboy"

The Greensboro Review: "Black Girl," "Pather Panchali"

The Harvard Review: "Run Lola Run"

Michigan Quarterly Review: "Do the Right Thing," "One Week," "The Red Balloon," "Westworld"

The New England Review: "Ikiru," "Stranger Than Paradise"

Poets.org: "Un Chien Andalou"

Unicorn Press: "The Homesteader" (as a limited edition chapbook)

Virginia Quarterly Review: "Blazing Saddles"

Deepest gratitude also to the John Simon Guggenheim Foundation and the United States Artists Foundation for their generous support and encouragement.

Gratitude is also given for support, assistance with research, or simply encouragement from Michael Collier; Stacey D'Erasmo; Vievee Francis; Jonathan Freedman; Chantal Gibson; Linda Gregerson; Robert Havey, thanks for the slide show; Mitchell Jackson, thanks for the early edits; Marion and Dorothy Jones, thanks for the Black Classics film collection; Terry Kennedy; Vicki Lawrence; Adrian Matejka; Matthew Olzman; April Ossmann, for later edits; Benjamin Paloff; Charles Rowell; Keith Taylor; Lyrae Van Clief-Stefanon; and Leslie Wingard.

Special thanks to Jill Bialosky, Alison Liss, and Rebecca Schultz for making this one possible. And thanks, still, to Carol Houck Smith for the conversation from which "The Homesteader" emerged.

The epigraph from *Tragic Sense of Life* comes from the version translated by J. E. Crawford Flitch.

Metropolis. This German Expressionist film from 1927 carries a fuller narrative in its restored edition. The infatuation of Freder (Gustav Fröhlich) with Maria (Brigitte Helm) leads him into the catacombs of the plant with the workers; this is fleshed out more in the restored edition. His quest for Maria fuels his new quest to save the workers from their drudgery, and, in the process, coming into his own as a man, stepping out of the shadow of his autocratic father. The night I saw this in Ann Arbor, MI, the line was literally wrapped around the block; the movie started thirty minutes late to accommodate the crowd; you don't want people filing in late during a silent film. There was a live organist in a tuxedo, and the audience was completely rapt, reading intertitle cards and listening to queues from the organist. It made the moviegoing experience a live event, a performance.

Stranger Than Paradise. That Jim Jarmusch is from my hometown of Akron, OH, always amused me; I not only understand from where his quirky style emanates, but I also respect the permission he allows himself for it to thrive. Though this wasn't my favorite film of his—*Down by Law, Mystery Train, Ghost Dog, Broken Flowers*, still favorites—but I do love what this film adds up to. The dramatic irony is that these characters are on a quest, whether they realize it or not. This is realism, though; most people are unwittingly on a quest, but we so often dismiss it as fate. This film presents a voyeur's view of this journey.

Last Year at Marienbad. Every time I see this film, I get something new out of it. This alone makes it one of my favorites. That every frame of it is composed with the keen eye of a still photographer only makes it more seductive. Games of chance, reverie, innuendo, infidelity, and the magnetism of attraction all factor in prominently in its composition. If one thinks the man who approaches this woman asking if she remembers sleeping with him last year—at this same soirée, in this same château—is inappropriate, one need only watch a bit longer to question whether he's the predator or the prey. Like a good poem, we only need to raise the question and think about its implications. Who needs an answer?

The Red Shoes. Though it's true that obsession can be fatal, it's also true that to fight for something or someone you love may make life worth living. Maybe that's the moral to this story: When Vicky (Moira Shearer) begins her dance, it's clear that she's in love with the life she's dancing; that is to say, for Vicky, life *is* dancing. And when Lermontov (Anton Walbrook) and later Julian (Marius Goring) see Vicky, we know what each man loves in this world. And we also begin a story that transcends the original fairy tale of Hans Christian Andersen. It becomes a fairy tale, albeit a grim one, for adults.

Nosferatu. Shadows have never been used to greater effect than in this film. The possibility of what Orlok/Nosferatu—Dracula, really, but Murnau didn't secure the rights to Bram Stoker's novel, so he changed the name—could do with the embodiment of what lay behind the shadows always felt scarier than watching his gore play out. I think there's a bit of the antihero in us all, and there's always an antidote to allow that part to go unchecked. Here, Orlok gets so enthralled with the beauty (and the blood) of Ellen that he drinks from her vein into the sunrise, which, of course, kills the vampire. He chooses his demise by choosing to give himself over to his desire. And if you have to choose a way to go . . .

Un Chien Andalou. I won't pretend to understand this film, Salvador Dalí, or Luis Buñuel, but I do understand how it makes me feel when I see it: that the mysteries of life and love are cyclical. Whether birth or death or love, everything takes time to be revealed.

Killer of Sheep. Being in the struggle of life is often more compelling than having it all figured out. Watching the adult characters in this film *try* at life is almost as beautiful as watching the children in the film play. You realize that the adults struggling were once these kids, and their ability to play as children is what keeps their spirits buoyed as adults.

The Mack. Most people see this as just another blaxploitation film with a pimp, but I think Max Julian brings a lot to this anemically written role. What strikes me about this film, though, are the scenes in which Goldie (Max Julian), the pimp protagonist, has conversations with and about his mama (Juanita Moore, of *Imitation of Life* fame). Ultimately, the entire plot hinges upon this relationship; every decision he finally makes emanates from the danger he puts his mother in. He, ultimately, must stop sacrificing the safety of the women he "employs," too. It's not until he starts seeing women as something other than pawns in a game that he begins to change his life.

Pather Panchali. Watching a child grow up is compelling enough, but watching a child grow up while overcoming insurmountable odds just makes you want to embrace all children. This is particularly the case once you see the aftermath of losing one child and the gift of having another child survive. *Pather Panchali* is part of a neorealist trilogy, *The Apu Trilogy*, which poses the question of what are the skills you need when you leave your father's house. But this is no prodigal son. Apu, from childhood to manhood, shows how it's done.

M. Peter Lorre has a face that calls for sympathy, even on a good day. In this film, even playing child murderer Hans Beckert, the sympathy comes as he tries to control himself. Later, he tries to escape vigilante justice from other criminals in Berlin. At one point when captured, he says, "Who knows what it's like to be me?" Although I have no idea, thankfully, what this urge feels like in a murderer, we all have subjective realities we live and try to defend.

Rififi. Whenever anyone talks about this film, they always reference the thirty-minute heist scene that has no dialogue; it's men at work on a highly skilled job. But what surprises me is how badly these guys behave. The misogyny is high; the lifestyle is fast and reckless. By the end, we see that this behavior may be rewarded all too often, but bad boys sometimes get their comeuppance.

The Great Train Robbery. When this film first played in theaters in 1903—the first Western, all of twelve minutes long—the scene in which Bronco Billy points his gun directly at the camera and shoots made audience members scream and duck under their seats. It's not only hard to imagine a new art form in the twenty-first century, but it's also hard to imagine any art form having the immediate influence on the public that film had at the turn of the twentieth century.

The Brother from Another Planet. You can look like the people in a new community, you might even be accepted by them, but you always know you're not from their world. The Brother (Joe Morton) is an escaped slave from another planet, he lands in Harlem, NY, and, though he looks like everyone around him, he also doesn't quite fit in. After a while, though, the community around him—and the brother from another planet, himself—realizes that they have a common experience (and enemy) in their universe of oppression.

The Homesteader. Oscar Micheaux's life story is greater than the plot of most films. An autodidact to the core, he went from working as a Pullman porter to tilling land as a homesteader in South Dakota, to writing novels and selling them door-to-door, to making films. Did I mention that this is a black man in the 1910s? There's no extant copy of *The Homesteader*; it's an adaptation of Micheaux's roman à clef by the same name. But of what we know, like most artists, his life informed his art. He was obsessed with racial uplift, fighting injustice, Booker T.

Washington, and financial security. The Leo (*Frank*) *v.* (*State*) Mary Phagan trial was another obsession. During this trial, for the first time, black "witnesses" were used to convict an ostensibly white (Jewish) defendant. Local blacks were threatened by white men emboldened by the resurgence of the Ku Klux Klan: they either testified that this Jewish man killed this young white woman, or these men, calling themselves the *Knights of Mary Phagan*, would burn them out of their homes or do worse to their families. Micheaux saw their testimony as selling out. In many of his films, the subplot is of a "race traitor" informing whites of the plans of blacks. The race traitor always gets his comeuppance in a Micheaux film, though. When Leo Frank's body was brought back to New York—he was from Brooklyn, but he moved south to manage a pencil factory in Milledgeville, GA— the *New York Times* reported that a "Negro sophisticate" was in Penn Station with the crowd to memorialize Frank. They had no name for this well-dressed African American man in the crowd, we have no copy of *The Homesteader*, and I thought what if that was Micheaux in the crowd that day. It's pretty unlikely that it was, but it's pretty clear he was with Frank in spirit. So, I thought, why not bring them together here.

Do the Right Thing. The story takes place over the course of one day in Brooklyn, but all the characters have history; this is just the day that all of the history comes to a head. Spike Lee—and, while I'm at it, John Sayles—doesn't get enough credit for putting characters in dialogue, honestly, across racial and cultural lines. These characters say what everyone on the street is thinking. This movie renders what would happen if our thought clouds were burst in mixed company.

Run Lola Run. Who hasn't performed stupid acts for love? Lola (Franka Potente) tries to help her boyfriend, Manni (Moritz Bleibtreu), out of a jam. Manni loses and now needs to replace $100,000 that belongs to a drug lord; he has twenty minutes to find the money. Lola tries and tries and tries, repeating her series of efforts as if caught in the movie *Groundhog Day*. That they keep trying makes this worth watching again and again and again.

I've Heard the Mermaids Singing. Unrequited love never looked sweeter than in this film. Polly (Sheila McCarthy) is well meaning but a bit hapless and socially awkward. She has mostly worked as a temp because she just can't seem to get the hang of anything. Yet, she seems to have some facility with photography. She falls for a woman much more sophisticated than she: Gabrielle (Paule Baillargeon), who curates a gallery at which Polly finally lands a job. Gabrielle is not only out of Polly's league, but she's also involved with another sophisticated woman. Is it possible for someone like Polly to ever win a Gabrielle? Who cares? We just want to see Polly give it a try, and she goes for it.

Black Girl. Diouana (Mbissine Thérèse Diop) is one of those characters you fall in love with as soon as they enter the story. Diop is one of those actors you want to stare at for a couple of hours, easy. So this is an equation for emotional investment—if not unbridled infatuation, at least—woven into the writing and casting. Sembène takes it further by framing Diop beautifully in every scene, whether close-ups in cramped interiors or long tracking shots outside. The story of how the dignified Diouana is tricked into moving from Dakar to Antibes to work as an au pair, only to find later that the young white French couple really wanted her to work as a live-in maid, is already a tragedy of spirit, which we witness for most of the film. The surprising yet logical ending of this film restores agency in our hero.

American Gigolo. When I saw this movie in the theater as a teenager, I knew I was watching something that I'd never forget. At the time, however, I had no idea *why* I wouldn't forget it. Looking at it now, I think Richard Gere's Julian was the first male hero I saw on film who was truly vulnerable while maintaining style, tenacity, and swagger. He was a real man with a real problem. That is to say, neither Steve McQueen nor Clint Eastwood could have played this role with the sincerity Gere brings to this male sex worker, who looks for love in all the wrong places.

Blazing Saddles. It would be easy to call Mel Brooks a genius based on his comedic writing alone, but it would also be a disservice to his level of craft. This film, like many of Brooks's films, delves into social politics like no other American filmmaker, whether that filmmaker is primarily dramatic or comedic in approach. This film—like Brooks's version of *To Be or Not to Be*, which he wrote, produced, and acted in, and which, in my opinion, holds up better over time than Ernst Lubitsch's original—not only handles the politics of race in the midseventies, but it also tackles the politics of sexual orientation. These are two tough subjects for people to talk about; that he is able to make us think about them *and* to laugh through the thinking is, well, genius.

Westworld. This is a story about what goes wrong when we get to live out our fantasies without a "safe word." Set in an amusement park for adults that replicates the Old West—and ancient Rome, and the Renaissance—something goes wrong with the lifelike robots in the brothel and the saloon. The sex workers say no and the gunslingers shoot back. Once the robot workers have agency, the consequences are as grave as they would be in the real world. As fun as it sounds to live out our fantasies with impunity, it's also fun to watch as they get reined in and as those among us who resist tempering get their comeuppance.

The Cabinet of Dr. Caligari. This German Expressionist film has one of the first twist endings in film. Dr. Caligari and his faithful somnabulist, Cesare, are accused of a series of murders in a German mountain community. At the end, we find out that our narrator, Francis, is really a delusional mental patient; his delusion is that the head of the asylum, Dr. Caligari, and another patient, Cesare, are the serial killers. Once Francis's delusion is revealed to Caligari, he realizes that he can now cure Francis. I saw this one in a theater with a live organist; I remember feeling a bit dazed, like Francis, or a bit like the sleepwalker. But I couldn't stop thinking that understanding what we're deluding ourselves about is half the battle. So, in this way, I was fully awake.

Ikiru. After thirty years of service in a government job and after learning he has stomach cancer and a few months to live, Kanji Watanabe (Takashi Shimura) chooses to do one meaningful deed before he dies: he completes the paperwork to build a playground in a poor neighborhood, where a cesspool is making life harder for the citizens. It's sad to think of a bureaucrat giving his entire life to work—no vacations, no sick days—and no play, but it's something transcendent to think of this worker choosing to do one meaningful thing before he dies. This is more than most people can say about their jobs or their lives, but it's beautiful when those who are most underestimated find meaning in both, even if just for a few months.

The Red Balloon. The metaphor of the red balloon is so perfectly elegant that even a child can understand it. Lamorisse wisely cast his son Pascal in the lead role, as a boy named Pascal who finds a red balloon; the balloon soon takes on the personality of a secret friend. Pascal believes the balloon embodies a will, soon the other kids recognize what Pascal has in this new friend, and their jealousies get the best of them. Pascal, emboldened by the power of belief, rises above them—literally and figuratively. If you can't relate to this story, I feel sorry for you.

One Week. When life looks good for you—when you have money, you have love, you have a home—someone is always going to be jealous. And sometimes they will even try to ruin your good time. Buster Keaton's character is not discouraged by the small act of jealousy that turns his world upside down in this story. In fact, he's unflappable as he keeps forging ahead against the forces against him. How can anyone resist cheering him on?

Oldboy. There's a surprise in every scene of this film. In fact, I think this is the case for every film I've seen by Park Chan-Wook. Nonetheless, there's also the familiarity of the human condition. In this film, the big mystery is what did the protagonist, Oh

Dae-su (Choi Min-sik), do to his high school friend, Woo-jin (Yu Ji-tae), who has set out to get revenge in the most elaborate and sadistic way imaginable. No, it's really unimaginable, but the suspension of disbelief is too strong to resist; the equation of the acting, writing, and direction of this film makes everything possible.